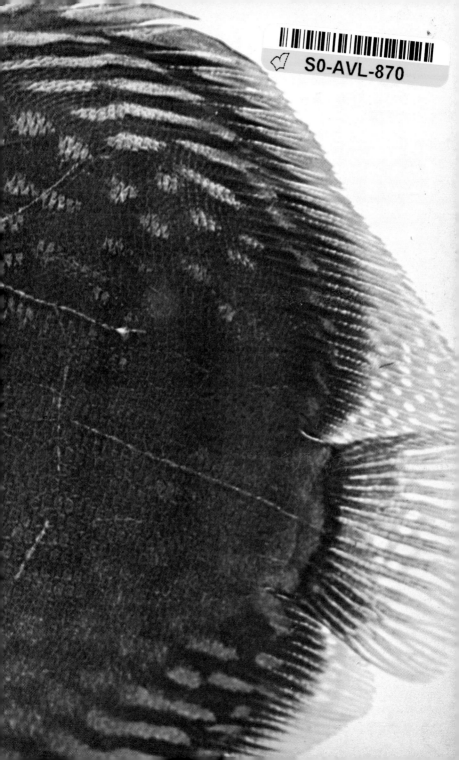

CONTENTS

Covers: A brown discus, *Symphysodon aequifasciata axelrodi*, feeding on tubifex worms.

Endpapers by Dr. Herbert R. Axelrod.

Frontis: The high dorsal fin of the discus earns it the name pompadour fish. Photo by M. Kocar.

ISBN 0-87666-535-0

© 1980 by T.F.H. Publications, Inc.

Distributed in the U.S. by T.F.H. Publications, Inc., 211 West Sylvania Avenue, PO Box 427, Neptune, NJ 07753; in England by T.F.H. (Gt. Britain) Ltd., 13 Nutley Lane, Reigate, Surrey; in Canada to the pet trade by Rolf C. Hagen Ltd., 3225 Sartelon Street, Montreal 382, Quebec; in Southeast Asia by Y.W. Ong, 9 Lorong 36 Geylang, Singapore 14; in Australia and the South Pacific by Pet Imports Pty. Ltd., P.O. Box 149, Brookvale 2100, N.S.W. Australia; in South Africa by Valid Agencies, P.O. Box 51901, Randburg 2125 South Africa. Published by T.F.H. Publications, Inc., Ltd, the British Crown Colony of Hong Kong.

DISCUS

TONY SILVA AND BARBARA KOTLAR

Because of its extreme lateral compression, a discus can easily maneuver in and out of clusters of tall plants; such plants, artificial or real, make a nearly ideal environment for a discus aquarium. Photo by Andre Roth. **Below:** While breeding pairs of discus seem to prefer solitude, discus are by and large gregarious fish that thrive well in large groups in a large aquarium. Photo by A.L. Pieter.

Introduction

Much can be said about the mystique of the discusfishes, which have fascinated and perplexed man ever since the first discus was introduced to modern aquarists in 1933. From that time until now discusfishes have captured the interest of scientists and hobbyists alike, although oddly enough the first discus species, described by Dr. Johann Heckel in 1840, had not attracted much attention.

The natural habitat of the discusfishes is the Amazon region of South America. They are cichlids, members of the family Cichlidae. They have a pancake shape and usually range in size from five to six inches.

There is a controversy over the classification of discus, and it is not the aim of this book to solve this problem. Some

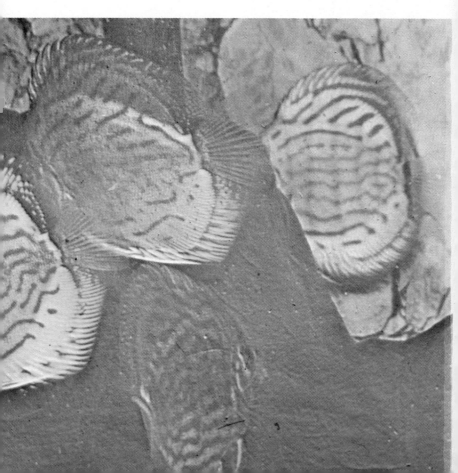

ichthyologists believe that there are two species, *Symphysodon discus* and *Symphysodon aequifasciata*, with *S. aequifasciata* having a number of subspecies. Others maintain that all discus should be grouped together. *Symphysodon*, incidentally, means "having teeth in the middle of the jaw."

It is the hope of the authors that this book will serve as a guide for beginning aquarists. There is still much to be learned about the physical as well as the psychological traits of these fishes. It is a challenge well worth undertaking. Some hobbyists might have opinions which differ greatly from those of the authors. This is true in any field, especially in the realm of keeping tropical fishes. Improved techniques and treatments must keep on being developed if discus are to maintain their real stature—for no less can be done for a fish that can rightly claim the honor of being called "the king of the aquarium."

←1

2

The photos on these two pages clearly demonstrate the most distinguishable difference between *Symphsodon aequifasciata* and *S. discus.* (1) *S. aequifasciata* has numerous vertical bars (Photo by G. Senfft). In *S. discus* (2) the eye bar, midbody bar and caudal peduncle bar; are most prominent; photo by Mueller-Schmida. (3) Even young *S. aequifasciata* show the prominent multi-bar pattern. Photo by G. Marcuse.

3

The best time for collecting wild discus is at night. A flashlight must be either held in the mouth or strapped to the head so that both hands are free to capture the discus, which are found around masses of sunken trees and roots. Photo by Dr. Herbert R. Axelrod. **Below:** While wild discus are usually quite colorful, selective breeding by aquarists has produced even more colorful strains like these, which were developed by Dr. E. Schmidt-Focke. Photo by A.L. Pieter.

Collecting Wild Discus

Collecting wild discus is an adventure in itself. The natural habitat of the discus is the backwater system of the Amazon in Brazil, Colombia, Peru and possibly Venezuela. The discus inhabits small *igarapes* or *lagos* (creeks and lakes) that branch off from the turbulent, swift-flowing Amazon. Here the water is shallow, slow-moving, clear or dark, loaded with submerged tree branches, trunks and roots that provide security and a natural protection for the discus school.

It is next to impossible to collect discus without the help of a native fisherman, usually an Indian. He provides not only the boat but also the necessary knowledge of the location of igarapes that might be laden with discus. The fisherman waits until nightfall before he sets out to collect the fish; the

discus usually move to the water's surface. The native uses a flashlight to blind the fish momentarily. He must net the fish quickly before he loses it. If he is fortunate, he will collect one fish per boat per hour. Discus are also caught when they leave the river for creeks. The Indian places a net around a small tree trunk or fallen tree and proceeds to chop the tree and remove the branches. The native then entraps the discus individually in a net. This method sometimes proves very successful, capturing a whole colony of discus.

After the fisherman returns to his village, he stores the fish in net traps until a motorized boat takes the discus to Belem or Manaus (Brazil), Iquitos (Peru) or Leticia (Colombia). Brown discus usually come from the Belem area, blues and Heckels from Manaus, and greens from Iquitos and Leticia.

The color and condition of the discus determine their price. Usually the native receives fifty cents to a dollar for each specimen. It is not uncommon for the least desirable discus to end their days in the skillet of the native.

While the fish are awaiting shipment to other countries, they are fed beefheart and brine shrimp. When the time arrives for transport, the discus are bagged singly. Then the bag is wrapped in newspaper and placed in a second bag, followed by another bag. The newspaper keeps the spines of the fish from piercing the bag. The fish are then shipped to distributors, usually in New York or Florida for the U.S. market. From there the fish go to warehouses all over the country until buyers from pet shops purchase them.

During this period some of the discus will die as a result of water and temperature changes. Often the discus will go on a hunger strike and refuse to eat, since they have not been fed for awhile. These complications reduce the number of originally healthy fish. Diseases also take a toll.

SPECIES AND VARIETIES OF DISCUS
The **Heckel** discus (*Symphysodon discus* Heckel) comes from the soft, acid waters of the Rio Negro near Manaus,

Brazil. The fish gets its name from Dr. Johann Heckel, who made its identity known to the world in 1840. The background color of the Heckel is composed of blue and reddish horizontal alternating bands. They have a wavy, irregular appearance; they originate on the forehead and behind the operculum, ending at the caudal fin. The head and body are crossed by nine vertical bars. Three of the nine vertical bars are very dominant; the others are almost invisible. The first prominent bar runs through the eye, the second through the middle part of the body and the third through the base of the caudal fin. The central black bar is the broadest and most pronounced. The anal and dorsal fins are tinged with red. Usually the eyes are red, which is characteristic of discus in most cases.

Since pure Heckels are very rarely spawned in captivity, crosses are more readily available. Almost all the crosses will have the three black bars.

The **brown** discus (*Symphysodon aequifasciata axelrodi* Schultz, 1960) was named after Dr. Herbert R. Axelrod, who has made numerous contributions to research on the discus. The fish comes from Belem at the mouth of the Amazon. The brown is characterized by a brownish background. Blue stripes extend through the head and dorsal and anal fins, which are edged in red. The nine vertical bars are evident throughout the body.

The **green** discus (*Symphysodon aequifasciata aequifasciata* Pellegrin, 1903) can be divided into two different types. The first is called Tefe green because it comes from Lake Tefe near the Amazon. It has a dark red-brown to golden background. Light and dark green stripes transverse the body. The fins are edged with red. The second type, the Peruvian green, is less colorful. Its background color is also red-brown to gold; there is a red edging on the fins. These discus gathered in Peru have red spots throughout the body. They are the hardiest of all wild discus.

The **blue** discus (*Symphysodon aequifasicata haraldi*

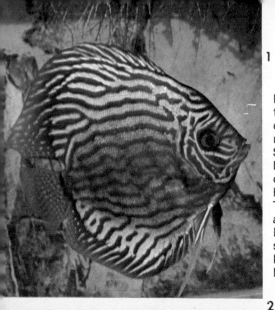

1

3 →

In the turquoise discus the fins and eyes show a concentration of red pigment. Photo by Dr. E. Schmidt-Focke. (2) The blue-brown-Heckel discus often shows the dark eye band and tail band. (3) The brown discus, *S. aequifasciata axelrodi*, lacks blue or green streaks on the body. Photos 2 and 3 by Andre Roth.

2

Schultz, 1960) is found near Manuas, Brazil. It resembles the brown. Almost the entire body is covered with short wavy blue lines. The anal and dorsal fins are edged in red.

The **powder blue** strain was developed by Mack Galbreath of Fresno, California. Males of this variety are entirely light blue, while the females are less colorful. There are light blue stripes in the face. The small amount of background color that is seen is red-brown. The fins are red.

The **turquoise** discus was named by Jack Wattley, a Florida breeder, who developed this variety. It is one of the most beautiful discus ever to grace the aquariums of the world. Mr. Wattley introduced the strain in 1969 after taking ten years to develop it. He crossed tank-raised royal blues with Lake Tefe greens that he had caught himself. The background color is a light brown. Turquoise-green stripes extend longitudinally across the body. The fins and eyes are predominantly red. The eyes are smaller than those of other discus.

The **red** discus is a colorful variety of the brown discus. The first specimens were caught near the Peruvian-Brazilian border. They were bred in Germany and were sometimes called the "red gypsy." The fins of these discus are a brilliant red. Their background is a reddish brown color.

Some discus appear to be red when they are first captured in the wild. According to some authorities, this red color is caused by the red dye emitted by a tropical fruit that sometimes falls into the water, adding red to any fish in the vicinity. Fishes so affected soon lose the color.

Brilliant turquoise is one of the many color variations of discus in the Amazon. The body has a mint-green color. The dorsal and anal fins are orange-red. These fish come from green-striped parents.

The **blue mask,** also called **blue face,** comes from crossing a brown and blue. It is characterized by blue lines running through the face and anal fin. The males are much more colorful than the females. The fins are edged in red. Occasionally, this discus might not have the blue lines in the face.

Hong Kong blues are offspring of greens and browns. Males have a few lines running through the face and the dorsal and anal fins. Females look like the browns but have a bit of blue on the dorsal and anal fins.

The **royal blue** was developed from blue males that were dominant in the wild discus colonies. Only one in a hundred might be found. The dominant males should be used to enhance or develop new variations. The background color is mahogany, and blue stripes go across the body. The body fins are edged in red.

The **solid blue** strain was developed by Dr. Edward Schmidt-Focke from Jack Wattley's stock. They are solid blue with red dorsal and anal fins.

The **cobalt** (Heckel royal blue) was developed by Dr. C.V. Wall of California. It is characterized by the many blue-purple lines running horizontally through the body, which has a mahogany background. The fins are edged in red.

The **pompadour** discus (Heckel brown) is a cross which has the three vertical bars missing. Sometimes it will have a tinge of blue in the body and fins.

The **blue-brown Heckel** discus looks like a blue without the three black bars. It has eye-appealing light blue lines, and often a dark band is present through the face and tail.

The **LoBue albino** discus was discovered by Len and Silvia LoBue in California in a batch of royal blues. Fortunately, there was a pair, and every time the pair spawns a few more albinos are produced. The remainder are normally colored fry. These discus are most unusual in that they have pink eyes, a white body and a pink tinge in their stripes. They are most attractive and exotic.

The **long-fin-blue face red** has been developed in Asia. It was the experience of one of the authors that the fins of several of these fishes began disintegrating after a short time.

1

(1) The LoBue albino discus at nine months of age. This discus, like many other albino fishes, shows some blue and red pigment, but as always in an albino fish, the black pigment is missing. The albino strain is not yet being produced in large quantities. Photo by Alfred Castro. (2) This is a light form of the turquoise discus. Photo by A.L. Pieter. (3) A darker form of the turquoise discus. Both the light and the dark form show a considerable amount of red in the fins. Photo by H. Mayland.

2

3

COLOR VARIETIES FROM ASIA

In Southeast Asia thousands of discus are successfully spawned, especially *Symphysodon aequifasciata axelrodi*, the brown discus. Also offered by these breeders is a blue discus, which is really the result of a cross between the green discus *(Symphysodon aequifasciata aequifasciata)* and the brown discus. Even though the male has a few blue-green lines, these fish can never be compared to the blues or greens coming from Brazil. The female coloration is the same as that of the brown female. Heckel hybrids are marketed from this area but are inferior to the true Heckel coming from around Manaus, Brazil.

In Asia many breeders import thousands of wild discus and keep them in large tanks. Their food consists mainly of tubifex worms and mosquito larvae, both of which are inexpensive and plentiful. The fish are kept in rain water at a temperature of 80 to 86 degrees. One half of the holding tank's water is changed daily. As the discus pair off, they are separated from the rest and placed in 20- or 50-gallon tanks. They are kept in bare tanks with no aeration; only a container with tubifex is kept at the bottom. The discus are allowed to raise their fry, which are removed from the parents and placed in different tanks when they are four weeks old. These fry are fed newly hatched mosquito larvae or chopped tubifex. When the fry reach the size of a silver dollar, live daphnia and newly hatched brine shrimp become the mainstay of their diet. At approximately two months of age, these discus are shipped to Germany, the United States and other countries.

"Candyapple" is one of the newest strains of discus being imported from Southeast Asia. Fish of this strain have been administered testosterone to develop some blue in the face and then dyed to add a reddish tint to the body. The fish is really a brown discus *(S. a. axelrodi)*. A hormone-treated fish appears very colorful when purchased, but a few weeks later it loses its color totally.

The devious method of using hormones to pass off common discus to the unsuspecting hobbyist as a unique new strain of discus is becoming more widespread every year. That is just one reason why discus should be purchased only from a reputable dealer; if the buyer isn't careful, perhaps one day the turquoise or royal blue discus that are swimming so regally in his tank may turn out to be common browns. (A young brown will have a brownish hue to its body, whereas young colorful discus will have a light body.)

NEW DEVELOPMENTS

Many people in the United States and Germany are also spawning and raising discus. As a result, new strains are being developed—much to the delight of discus enthusiasts. There is definitely an art in breeding discus on a large scale. Several well-known breeders are successfully working in California and Florida. They must face the same problems a hobbyist faces—maintaining temperature, feeding proper food and fighting disease. These people are innovators in the discus world. The quality of discus in the future will be determined by how these new discus are being developed. New strains will hopefully be stronger and more disease-resistant.

A holding compound located near the Rio Negro in Brazil. Many beautiful discus strains had their origins in the black water of the Rio Negro.

(1) This fish has become known as Mack's powder blue discus. Photo by Mack Galbreath. (2) This blue discus lacks red pigment in the fins. Photo courtesy of *Midori-Shobo* Magazine.

A breeder usually has his own method for raising the fry artificially. By doing this, he can be sure a large number of fry will survive, thereby making it economically feasible for him to improve his methods and to become involved in further research. Discus obtained from these breeders are usually healthy, attractive fish with little exposure to parasites or bacteria.

Smaller breeders still have much to offer in the breeding field. Their knowledge and devotion often open new insights into the problems that plague the discus hobbyist. If the behavior patterns of the discus can be better understood, more steps can be taken to insure their survival. Any dedicated person can contribute to this goal, helping to make the discus a delight to raise.

Discus are shy fish if not kept in a suitable aquarium. The discus at the left appears to be right at home among the plant stems. Photo by H. Pinter. **Below:** Discus can be kept in a community aquarium if they are given enough room and plenty of ribbon-like plant clusters into which they can retire from the activities of the other fishes in the tank.

Aquarium Environment

In order for discus to thrive and develop properly, a well-planned aquarium set-up should be utilized. It is impractical to duplicate the backwaters of the South American rivers, but an adequate substitute can be provided.

Thirty-gallon tanks can hold up to two dozen adolescent discus. As the fish reach maturity and choose a mate, however, it is best to place each "pair" in a 20-gallon tank, which is the size recommended by most breeders. (Because of the water changes and temperature requirements, 50-gallon tanks are not practical.) Regardless of the size of tank used, each tank should be equipped with a good full-hood reflector.

←1

2

(1) Creating the best environment for discus means using thick clusters of tall plants like these *Vallisneria gigantea*. Photo by Dr. D. Terver, Nancy Aquarium, France. (2) The lateral compression of the discus allows it to slip in and out of thickets of tall thin plants quite easily. Photo by Andre Roth. (3) The vertical barred pattern of the discus provides it with good camouflage among reedy plants or sunken tree branches.

3

Aquarium placement is quite important to the habits and temperament of the discus. Many discus keepers go to extremes and place their discus in a dark corner away from all other fish and people where no one can see or bother them. Some pet shops place their discus tanks on very high racks where no one can tap on the glass, for example. The discus tank can be kept out in the open so long as it is in a relatively quiet surrounding. The active pursuits of children, dogs and cats should not be allowed near a discus tank. These actions will make the discus scared and nervous. Nothing should ever be thrown into the water, and quick movements should be avoided. It is best to keep the discus about four feet from the floor, thus enabling the fish to view a person fully.

It is necessary to keep the tank scrupulously clean from the moment it is utilized. Gravel and pebbles are very attractive but can be detrimental to the health of the discus. Uneaten food and waste matter lodge in the gravel, unleashing bacteria and parasites. What a keeper gives up in appearances by not having gravel in the tank is made up for by increased ease of cleaning the tank. Artificial plants, especially the Amazon sword plant, are most suitable for decoration and can easily be removed and cleaned.

Discus do exceptionally well with a frequent water change, since changing the water helps destroy harmful bacteria and will increase the appetite of the fish. Removal of one-fourth of a tank of water each week is advised. Replace this with regular tap water. It is not necessary to age the water. The chlorine in the water dissipates in several hours. Be sure the replacement water is the same temperature as that of the tank or a couple of degrees higher. Use different equipment in cleaning a community tank so that diseases cannot be transferred from one to the other. These water changes are especially desirable for young fish, since they will eat better and their intestines can function properly. Some mated pairs refuse to spawn unless given a water change. Frequent water changes are beneficial for all fishes; not only harmful bacteria but also waste products are removed.

It is advisable to discover what chemicals are being added to the water in your area. Try to discover whether the amounts are variable. One day the authors lost nine adolescent blues because the water change had contained a higher amount of chlorine than usual because of a storm that had churned up muck in Lake Michigan.

Keeping the filters clean is important in maintaining a healthy discus tank. Corner filters are very effective, and an outside filter can be used in addition. Also periodically wash off any other items utilized in the tank as well as the sides.

Discus do not thrive well in community tanks. Many other fishes cannot tolerate the higher temperatures that discus prefer. They will also become a nuisance to the discus by quickly devouring the food and by swimming nervously in the tank. Some fishes (a few of the barbs are good examples) will nip the fins of the discus. Angelfish blend beautifully with the discus to all appearances, but combining them is a mistake, since angels can carry a worm (genus *Capillaria*) that can be fatal to a discus. Peaceful fishes such as *Uaru* and *Corydoras* can be good tank companions. If other fishes are to be used in the discus tanks, choose species that can thrive on higher temperatures and that are peaceful.

Discus must be kept at a temperature range of 79° to 84° F. or more. Heckels must be kept in waters from 85° to 90° F., since they come from warmer waters. The discus in their native habitat in South America live in slow-moving, soft, acid waters with a temperature of 79 to 84 degrees. Often discus are captured in shaded creeks in which the water temperature is lower. However, these discus are usually skinny and have fin fungus. Discus are healthier in warmer water. Never allow the temperature to drop below 79° F., since this change will cause the discus to become sickly or to go on a hunger strike. An increase in temperature can break a hunger strike and is beneficial in treating the discus for

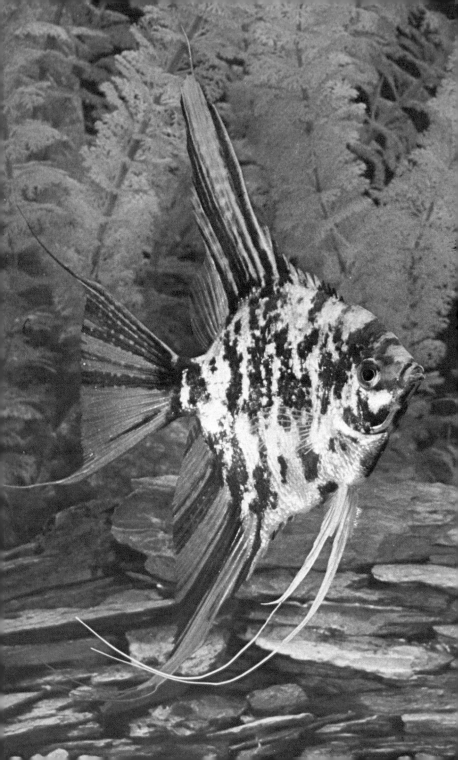

←1

2

(1) Like discus, angelfish also have a laterally compressed body and a tendency toward vertical barring. Photo courtesy of Wardley Products Co. (2) A few *Corydoras* catfishes should be kept in the discus tank to pick up uneaten food that may settle on the bottom. Photo by H.J Richter. (3) Another good tankmate for discus is the uaru, *Uaru amphiacanthoides,* which is also a shy and peaceful fish and thrives in a similar environment. Photo by H. Azuma.

3

worms. Some breeders find that lowering the temperature to 79° F. will condition the female discus to develop eggs.

Discus fare best in soft water, 2 to 4 DH on the German hardness scale. This is the range in which they live in the Amazon waters of South America. The pH should range between 6.5 and 6.8; that is, a slightly acid condition of the water. Pure peat moss can be added to the filter to achieve the desired acidity in the tank.

SELECTING YOUNG DISCUS

When selecting young fish for breeding, show or simple enjoyment, the authors recommend that you choose a colorful variety. It is interesting to observe the growth of these discus, since their color develops during adolescence. Most of the young fish take about seven months before their colors become dominant. If a supposedly colorful discus does not color up, even though it's given proper care, chances are that it is a brown discus instead of a green. If so, the fish will never develop color.

The following is a brief description of some of the types of discus suitable to the desires and needs of a beginning discus fancier.

Browns, blue faces and reds are not very colorful fish. However, they are relatively inexpensive and can become the foundation of a discus community.

Blues (including royal blues, powder blues, blues, half blues and hybrids) are more colorful than the browns but are also more expensive.

Greens include greens, Tefe greens, turquoise and hybrids that have a green parent. Sometimes greens are sold as blues and blues as greens. Both types are strong and therefore for beginners; however, they are expensive.

Finally, there are the Heckels, the "original" discus. These fish should not be in a beginner's tank, since they require more care than other discus and are very shy. Also, very few breeders have spawned them so they are costly and rare. There are a few Heckel hybrids, such as a cobalt blue discus—which is a beautiful fish but, again, not recommended except for an advanced aquarist.

SHIPPING AND RECEIVING

If discus are to be shipped by air freight or air mail, there are several steps to follow to insure their physical well-being. If precautions are not taken, they will surely die from shock caused by changes of water temperature and drastic pH and hardness changes. Do not feed the discus on the shipping day. A 25% water change in their tank should be made, using 75% aged water and 25% tap water. To do this, add some type of product designed to acclimate fish to changed conditions; your dealer will be able to recommend a suitable product. Fill a large plastic bag a quarter full with water. More oxygen is desirable than water. Place the fish in the quarter-filled bag and fill the rest of the bag with pure oxygen. Tie the bag with several rubber bands and cover this bag with a newspaper. Place the bag inside another bag. This bag should now be placed inside a Styrofoam shipping box and then inside a cardboard box. Six small discus can be shipped in a plastic bag. Two of these bags are then placed in the Styrofoam container.

The person to whom the fish are being sent should be notified concerning the time, flight number and company which is handling the transport. On the top of the shipping box, write the name and address of the person receiving the fish and also their phone number. Make a notation for the company to call them upon arrival. Also place your name and address on the package.

Shipping the discus by air mail will help the fish arrive at their destination sooner. The fish should be bagged singly with plenty of pure oxygen. Follow the above procedure.

Upon receiving fish, remove them from their shipping container as soon as possible. Add a cup of water from the tank to the bag while floating the bag on top of the tank. Add

1

These photos of the natural habitat of the discus make it easy to understand why wild-caught discus are not that frequently available. The jungle thickets make the habitats difficult to get to, and many of the habitats are accessible only during the part of the year when the waters are high. Photo 1 by H. Schultz. Photos 2 and 3 by Dr. Herbert R. Axelrod.

34

2

3

1

Full, rounded bodies and well rounded foreheads are signs that **2** discus have been eating well and are in good health. Discus having a hollow or drawn appearance around the eyes should not be purchased. Photo 1 by G. Budich. Photo 2 by M. Kocar.

one cup every twenty minutes for three hours. This helps the temperature, pH and hardness to be equalized with the water in the tank. Do not feed the discus the day they are received (they probably will not eat anyway.) Do not feed adult discus for two days. Some discus will actually take two weeks before they will begin eating in their new surroundings.

Fish that have not been packed for shipping properly will float sideways on top of the tank and have ragged, broken fins. If the fish survive, the fins will correct themselves in several days. Be wary of dealing with people who do not ship discus in the proper manner, for a great deal of money and time can be lost.

Compare the dark-colored discus in photos 1 and 2 with the light-colored discus in photo 3. Dark overall color and clamped fins usually are signs that something is wrong. Photo 1 by Dr. Herbert R. Axelrod. Photo 2 by H. Schultz. Photo 3 by M. Kocar.

2

39

White worms (enchytraeids) are a highly nutritious food for discus, but they must not be fed to the fish too often, for an excess of them can cause some digestive problems. Photo by E. Stansbury. **Below:** White worms are easily cultivated in a wooden or plastic box containing a mixture of garden soil and loam. Photo by Robert Gannon.

Foods and Feeding

It is very important that discus be fed a variety of foods to keep them healthy and interested in what is offered to them. You have to remember that wild-caught adult discus have distinct food preferences. They won't, for instance, eat flake foods. Young discus will take it, especially if they were fed on it while they were very small, but wild adult discus will most certainly reject it. Some discus will eat freeze-dried tubifex worms, which is the only safe form of tubifex worms to feed the fish. The live tubifex worms come from sewage-ridden water filled with parasitic organisms and bacteria. By freeze-drying the worms, the majority of the undesirable elements are eliminated. It is highly probable that tubifex worms are a contributing factor in the most dreaded discus disease, hole-in-the-head.

However, discus naturally enjoy devouring live foods, and there are several that can be considered safe. The first are glass worms, not worms at all but actually fly larvae found under the ice in ponds. They are almost clear and about half an inch in length. Cleansing them in a fine mesh sieve in fresh water for half an hour is a must. Discus will reject any dead or sluggish ones but will readily digest the lively glass worms with gusto. The worms must be kept in a plastic container filled with water at a temperature between 45 to 60 degrees.

White worms are another food source to include in the diet. These worms can be bred by obtaining a culture from the fish shop. They must be stored in a tightly covered container filled with peat moss and humus. Oatmeal, mashed potatoes or bread soaked in milk should be added every few days. The temperature must be kept in the middle 50's for best results. The worms will die at 75 degrees. It is most important to cleanse these worms before feeding to the discus.

In general, discus fanciers need a food that the fish will enjoy and benefit from and that cannot transfer any harmful organisms to the discus. One of these is frozen beefheart, which is a nutritionally sound source of food. Frozen beefheart can be purchased in pet shops, and buying it in pet shops is the most sensible arrangement for small-scale users. Large-scale users, however, often process their own. Beefheart can be obtained from a butcher. It must always be fresh, since the defrosting/re-freezing process can promote the growth of harmful bacteria. All fat and gristle must be cut from the heart. If ten pounds are utilized, only five pounds will remain after the fat and gristle have been removed. Then the cut meat must be processed through a food grinder, *not* a blender. Prepare a mixture of the following. First, dissolve an adult vitamin and mineral capsule in a cup and a half of boiling water. Use one cap sule for every five pounds of processed meat. Add a tablespoon of agar-agar and three envelopes of plain gelatin. Bring this mixture to a boil and then force through a sieve. Immediately add this mixture to the ground beefheart. Mix thoroughly. Divide the beefheart into small portions and place in plastic bags. Flatten the mixture in the bags so that a piece can be cut off easily after it is frozen. A knife can be used to cut the beefheart for large discus, and a razor blade can shave off small amounts for smaller discus.

If beefheart is to be made at home, a variation can be substituted occasionally. For each pound of ground beefheart mixture, add a quarter pound of liver. Grind once more and add one egg yolk. This preparation is high in cholesterol; therefore, it should be fed only once or twice a week.

There are several other food sources which are suitable to include in the discus diet. One of them is frozen brine shrimp. Even though approximately ninety percent of frozen brine shrimp is water, it does appeal to the discus' palate. The frozen brine shrimp should be placed in a small strainer and rinsed thoroughly so that the water it is suspended in will not be added to the tank and cloud the water. Brine shrimp can be hatched at home and fed to fry. These brine shrimp are very small and thus prove an unsatisfactory food for large discus.

Frozen daphnia can be included in the diet of the young discus. It can be purchased at a pet store. Mature fish seem to enjoy larger particles in a meal, so they do not relish these little pieces.

The diet of the discus is subject to many pros and cons. Every discus fancier has his own theory on which ingredients contained in a diet are most noteworthy. This book points out the food source that the authors believe is most beneficial to the discus—namely, beefheart, with its added protein, vitamins and minerals. Suitable worms can be included to vary the menu. If a fish is healthy, it will eat and will not require that exotic foods be served at each meal. Of course there is room for much experimentation on the part of the hobbyist as to which foods in the diet are superior. Of course, such tests are done at the expense of the discus. It is essential that the discus receives the correct nutrients necessary to maintain its best physical condition.

Vitamins supposedly increase the appetite and induce early development of the discus. There are various brands on the market available either in tablet or liquid form. The B vitamins are the main ingredients. The label should be carefully read before administering to the fish. Never purchase vitamins that contain hormones. This will artificially improve the color of the fish but can be detrimental to the discus and possibly to the person who dispenses them.

In order to maintain conditions necessary for promoting optimum growth and health, the hobbyist should adopt a strict routine for feeding the discus. Adult fish should be fed twice daily, preferably at the same time each day. Only an amount of food that can be consumed in several minutes should be placed in the tank. Chop or shave any large particles of food to facilitate the process of eating. Any food not consumed must be removed after each meal so that the water does not become fouled. The entire concept of frequent water changes and filters falls by the wayside when food is allowed to rot at the bottom of the tank, giving rise to undesirable bacteria.

It has been observed that some mature discus will indulge in self-imposed fasts. Usually discus will ravenously devour their food when fed. However, even though a fish might be healthy and not abused by his tank-mates, it might decide to stop eating. Many discus fanciers throw up their hands in despair when their large fish just watch the food sink to the bottom. There is some internal mechanism that regulates the time and quantity to eat. A discus might consume large amounts of food for several months and might even eat from your hand if you have gained its confidence—but then there will be a period of a couple of months during which it will fast and become sleek and trim. Just about the time a person decides the fish can no longer survive, the discus begins to eat again, looking none the worse for missed meals.

It has been observed that it is beneficial to the discus if the hobbyist fasts his fish one day a week after the fish are six weeks of age. This enables the digestive system to rid itself of any collected waste. The discus will have little trouble with constipation if this routine is followed. Choose the same day each week, and make the water change on that day. The fish will not begin a starvation diet; instead, they'll be more enthusiastic when fed the following day. A hobbyist will not encounter bloat when a fast regimen is adopted.

What to do with discus while on vacation is a problem which often arises. If no one will be present in the home while the hobbyist is away, the situation is not as critical as it might seem. About two weeks before the vacation will begin, lower the temperature gradually to 79°F. The day before the trip, make a 50% water change using tap water. Enlist the aid of a friend to come twice a week to feed the discus, giving them their favorite food. It is necessary to remove the food that is not eaten from the tank. If there is natural sunlight coming into the room it is not necessary to keep the tank light on. If the room is dark during the daytime, connect a timer to the light. This will help acclimate the discus to the change in schedule.

The discus will survive the absence of their owner; however, if the fish are being maintained for breeding, it must be pointed out that a change in schedule of this sort can possibly be a major setback.

CULTURING LIVE FOODS

Culturing food is not a difficult process, and it affords an excellent food source for the discus as well as other species. The following are descriptions of several live foods that can be cultured in your home.

Gammarus (crustaceans of the genus *Gammarus*) are small, about half an inch in length. They are a natural food for fish in the wild. They are often called scuds. Inexpensive cultures are obtainable from companies that advertise in fish magazines. Gammarus might appear under the name *Gammarus fasciatus* or *Gammarus pulex*.

These crustaceans live and breed in the dirty filter floss; because they ingest live and dead vegetation, they are classified as herbivorous. An aquarist can grow his culture in a pan with light aeration and filled with dirty fish water. Feed lettuce every three or four days. When the *Gammarus* are fed to the fish, remove the lettuce and shake off the animals into a clean cup of water. They should be kept in clean water for twenty-four hours before being fed to discus. The gammarus can aid in the digestion of the fish because they contain chitin. This food can be frozen and fed to the discus at a later time.

Bloodworms are larvae of midges of the genus *Chironomus*. They are very nourishing for the fish. The life cycle of the bloodworm has four stages: the egg, larva, pupa and adult. Obtain at least a dozen bloodworms from a dealer. Fill a gallon jug half full of aquarium water and place a small piece of Styrofoam in it for the midges to lay eggs on. The bottom should contain an eighth of an inch of white sand. Feed them yeast. Place screening over the top of the jug. Keep the temperature at 65° F. (The eggs will hatch in two or three days at 80° F.) When the eggs are laid, they will adhere with a gelatinous substance. Each egg case will be made up of about 500 eggs. The life span of an adult is only four or five days. The larvae can be kept in the refrigerator for several weeks; feed them to the fish when they are half an inch long.

Earthworms (*Lumbricus*, etc.) are a very good staple for fish. The smaller ones can be cut up and fed to discus, while the larger can be made into a paste in a blender to which a fourth of a teaspoon of agar-agar is added. Spread this mixture out to a thickness of a quarter of an inch. After it has solidified, cut it into sections and freeze. It can be fed to young as well as adult discus.

To culture these worms, an aquarist can use a Styrofoam shipping container filled with sifted garden soil or African violet potting soil. Place several dried leaves in the dirt. Feed the worms cereal, potatoes or crackers soaked in milk. The soil should remain moist, so cover it with a piece of cloth. The temperature should be kept at 65° F. After they are harvested, place the worms in peat so they can cleanse themselves.

Microworms are small, relatively colorless worms, usually about a sixteenth of an inch long. In a culture, there are 80% females. A culture multiplies quickly in several days, since these worms are livebearers. The worms are highly nutritious and serve the same purpose as brine shrimp nauplii when fed to the small discus. A culture can be purchased from a supplier or started from scratch. Cut a hole half an inch wide through a potato and bury it in the ground.After a week the potato should be full of microworms. They can then be cultured by using a waterproof shallow container which has a lid. A plastic shoebox will suffice. Use a high-protein cereal or oatmeal as a medium. Make a paste about a quarter of an inch thick and spread it on the bottom of the box. It should be kept at a temperature of about 70 to 75° F. Use the worms that climb onto the sides of the container. Replace the culture every two or three weeks, keeping only a tablespoon of the worms. Do not feed them yeast, since this substance can be harmful to the discus fry.

Whiteworms were introduced to the aquarium world in 1926. They belong to the family Enchytraeidae. These widely used worms range in size from one thirty-second of an inch to an inch. Whiteworms are an excellent fatty food which should be fed no more than three or four times a week to discus.

Since they are egg layers, they are easy to culture. Whiteworms are hermaphroditic (each individual contains

For your fish who love to eat

Produced for
fresh & salt
water species.

Tri-▲ SELECT
SUPLEMENTAL
SEAFOODS
The key in your
pet food chain.

Not for human consumption
Pet Food Only

Net Wt. 3 oz. - 85.05 gm. av.

A great variety of foods is important
to the health of discus. The diet
should include some frozen foods (1)
as well as an assortment of live
foods such as brine shrimp (2), *Gammarus* (3) and chopped or whole
small earthworms (4). Photo 3 by
Knaack. Photo 4 by P. Imgrund.

both sexes), so only several are necessary to start a colony.
Fill a Styrofoam container or plastic shoe box with African
violet potting soil that contains no fertilizer. Moisten the soil
and add a pinch of yeast and baking soda. The yeast adds
vitamins and the baking soda will keep the soil sweet-
smelling. The whiteworms can then be added. Then place a
thin layer of cooked oatmeal over the soil and place in the
dark at a temperature of 60° F. These worms will die at 70°
F. and will not breed at 35° F. When the worms can be seen
feeding, the harvest can begin. Put some of the dirt in hot
water, just deep enough to cover the bottom of the pile. The
worms will crawl to the top, where they can then be removed
with tweezers. Another method is to remove the top and bottom of a small can. Cover one end with screening and fill the
can with dirt. Use a clamp to attach the can (open end up) to
a stand. A dish of water should be placed about three inches
under the can. Turn a 25-watt bulb on above the can. The
worms will crawl through the dirt and screen and will then
drop into the water to escape the heat.

Grindal worms are a type of whiteworm that is smaller
than the more common whiteworms, thus making them an
ideal food for baby discus. They will not grow larger than
half an inch.

2

3

4

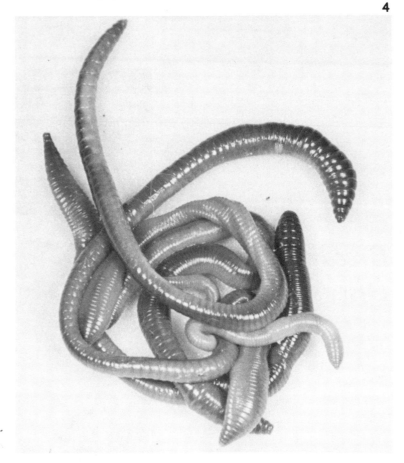

At the age of
six weeks, young discus
begin to strongly resem-
ble their parents in shape
and color pattern. Photo
by G. Wolfsheimer.
Below: Baby discus
feeding on skin secre-
tions of their parents.
Photo by G. Budich.

*Breeding
Discus*

SEXING DISCUS

If an aquarist were to purchase a group of large discus and a group of small discus that were spawned at the same time, he could assume that 90% of the large discus would be males and 90% of the small discus females. Many breeders claim to have hard and fast rules in discerning the sex of the fish, but we try to steer clear of "hard and fast" rules where sexing discus is concerned; we have found that not all methods work all of the time.

Often the sex can be determined by the formation of the lips and "nose." In an adult female discus, the lips are relatively the same size, whereas the upper lip of the male discus protudes. Additionally, in the male the "nose" is somewhat

(1) Discus prefer to lay their eggs on a vertical or near-vertical surface such as a swordplant leaf or the vertical edge of a large rock. Photo by G. Senfft. (2) Parent discus protectively hover over their offspring which have just hatched out of the eggs. (3) As soon as the fry are free-swimming they begin to feed on the parents' skin secretions. Photos 2 and 3 by G. Budich.

←1

2

3

crooked instead of straight. This observation is valid about fifty percent of the time.

The next method is used in determining the sex of browns. In these fish the blue of the anal fin extends into the body of the male. The female's blue coloration stays within the fin.

Another way of sexing the discus is to look at the formation of the anal fin itself. In the male the anal fin is straight while the female's is round. This sexing system is not foolproof, but it works about 70% of the time.

There are several other observations that are noteworthy in unraveling the puzzle. Usually the males are more colorful and their hues more vibrant throughout the body. The males are also the more aggressive fish. A male will reach the food first and will show his displeasure when another discus disrupts him in some manner.

The green discus are the easiest to sex; females have little color on the face and body, while the males are colorful all over.

Probably the most accurate way of determining the sex requires the removal of the discus from the water. The aquarist should first wet his hands. Next, catch the fish in a net and take hold of it gently. Use a magnifying glass and observe the breeding tube of the fish suspected to be the female. It will appear to be broader and rounder, while the male's is more pointed.

SPAWNING PREPARATIONS

One question asked concerning the discus mystique is what causes the discus to pair off and spawn. It is almost impossible to answer. Discus fanciers can only offer several plausible reasons for the activity.

In South America the discus spawn during the rainy season, which is characterized by constant rain, cooler water temperatures and changes in the length of the daylight period. The pH of the water rises to 6.5 from 4.5 or 5.5; that is, it becomes less acid. Since the lakes overflow from the torrential rains, the discus travel back to the creeks, where they join colonies near a sunken log or tree roots. The strongest discus have survived the dry season, during which the weaker ones succumbed to cold spells.

Some discus have been known to spawn as early as nine months of age, while others have been as old as four and a half years before they became interested in procreating. Usually browns spawn at a year of age, blues and greens at about eighteen months, and Heckels at about fifteen to twenty months. Most of the crosses and new strains will spawn at eighteen months.

There are several ways of obtaining mated pairs of discus. One is to purchase several adult wild discus and place them in a large tank with soft, acid water. Feed the discus live food. The temperature in the tank should be kept at 84° F. In a few months they begin to pair off. Once this feat is accomplished, remove the other fish from the tank. Do not remove the pair, since this disrupts the mating process. Finally, introduce a piece of slate or sterilized flower pot to set the stage for the pre-nuptial ritual. Another method is to purchase about eight small discus and raise them to the adult state. This way the fish will be accustomed to feedings and water quality from the beginning and will be more cooperative in pairing off and spawning.

If time is of the essence, a mated pair of discus can be purchased, usually with a very expensive price tag attached to the fish. Furthermore, they cannot be guaranteed to mate. Be aware of a few unscrupulous dealers who sell so-called "mated pairs" that are simply two discus thrown together without their sex even being known.

The best advice the authors can offer is to raise young discus and allow them to choose their own mates. Perseverance and patience are qualities a would-be breeder must develop if he is determined to be successful in breeding discus.

If the above methods of obtaining a mated pair fail, the

(1) A close-up of discus fry feeding on a parent's skin secretions. (2) When the fry are feeding on one parent, the other one often remains close by. (3) During the early feeding stages the young seldom wander far from the parents. (4) Feeding baby discus frequently swim as a group from one parent to the other. Photos by G. Budich.

3

4

hobbyist should try to duplicate the conditions of the Amazon as best he can. The temperature should be lowered from 84° F. to 79° F., and the pH should be increased to 6.5.More daylight hours should be provided and more frequent water changes made. The discus need live food such as brine shrimp, etc., in order to get them in condition for breeding. Hopefully, the discus will choose mates after these steps are taken.

It is not uncommon for two females to pair off and spawn, one spawning one week and the other the next. However, if the eggs are not fertilized, the conclusion must not be reached that the fish are both females, since some males will not fertilize during the first few spawns. If the aquarist is relatively certain he has two females spawning, it is best to separate them by placing them with other fish and hope they will choose a proper mate. This feat should be accomplished in a few weeks if all goes well.

Discus must be in prime condition if they are to spawn successfully. An overzealous aquarist does the fish an injustice by overfeeding it. Overfeeding not only is injurious to the fish's health but also makes it sluggish. The same can be said about an overly thin discus. The temperature should be raised to encourage eating so that some weight can be gained; hence, the pairing-off can eventually occur.

Once the discus have paired off they will separate from the group. The area around the head and tail will appear grayish. The fish will then swim toward one another, face downward, and then to the top of the tank while they are opening and closing their tail fins. They will next search for a suitable substratum for spawning. If there is not a piece of slate or a flower pot, they might choose a filter, thermometer, heater or even the side of the tank on which to spawn. When the choice is agreed upon, they will begin cleaning it with their mouths. They will do a shaking movement in front of the substratum. If one discus might stray away, the other will follow and shimmy in front of it.

Cleaning the surface in the preparation for spawning might take several hours or days. However, it is not that unusual to come across a pair that might take a month to complete this stage.

PARENTS AND FOSTER PARENTS

Many aquarists are of the opinion that discus will not raise their young themselves. There is some truth in that statement, especially when referring to tank-raised fish. Wild fish respond better to their paternal and maternal instincts.

If a pair of discus has spawned, and time or convenience does not allow for the discus to be raised artificially, let the parents raise the fish. The following procedure might work. Introduce a few large discus into the tank. Hopefully, the pair will continually keep the other fish from coming near the place where the eggs were laid. After the eggs hatch on the third day, insert a piece of glass close to where the wigglers are positioned so that the other discus do not have a chance to eat them. At this point, the pair might decide to eat the wigglers even though they might not have touched the eggs. If the fry have survived this far, they will begin feeding from the parents on the sixth day.

It is not unusual for a discus, whether wild or tank-raised, to claim sole jurisdiction over its new family and try to keep the other parent away. If this happens, allow the single parent to raise the batch and remove the other fish.

Fry that are raised on their parents are usually healthier: they grow faster and eat better and can produce a thicker slime themselves. Fry raised artificially will produce slime, but not as much. However, they have a tendency to refuse to raise their fry.

If the male eats the eggs while the female is laying them, break up the pair. Give him another opportunity by remating him. If the same conduct occurs, do not use this male for breeding. As a last resort, the fish might be fed at least seven times a day so that he will not become hungry enough to eat

(1) At two to three weeks of age discus fry will still feed on the parents' body slime even though they are fully capable of eating other foods such as newly hatched brine shrimp nauplii. Photo by G. Budich. (2) A two-month-old discus is still not as round in shape as its parents. Photo by L.E. Perkins.

the fry. This entails more work, since the tank must be kept clean of uneaten food.

The employment of foster parents in discus breeding is relatively rare, because often it is difficult to find a fish that will raise even its own young. However, if a breeder is fortunate enough to have a male or female with fry feeding from its sides, one can probably place the other fry with them so long as they are ready to feed from the parent. It shouldn't make any difference whether these fish are a few days younger than the others.

An aquarist can count his blessings if he has a female that generally does not eat her eggs or fry. The flowerpot on which the eggs were laid should be kept with the discus. Only one fish should be in the tank. It will begin to get darker because of the slime it is producing. On the fifth or sixth day the fry should begin to swim to its side to feed. Even though a fish might eat the eggs or fry one time does not necessarily mean it will happen again or vice versa. For unknown reasons, browns are more willing to raise a spawn than colorful fish, so if the breeder has a spawn of browns and turquoise, he can experiment by substituting the turquoise eggs for the brown. The brown discus might readily raise them.

Until recently, it was generally considered impossible to raise discus fry away from their parents, but within the last few years Jack Wattley and several other famous discus breeders have developed the proper food formula to make this possible. **Below:** A pair of blue discus guarding eggs which they have attached to a brick. Photo by Dr. Herbert R. Axelrod.

Raising Discus Fry Artificially

Years ago what was considered an impossibility is now quite a common occurrence. Many hobbyists who keep and breed discus are raising fry away from the parents. Mr. Jack Wattley of Fort Lauderdale was one of the first, if not the first, to raise discus in this manner. He spent six years endeavoring to discover a formula for raising discus fry away from the parent. He tried everything, logical and illogical. One day he found the secret formula. Another successful discus breeder was Mrs. Lois Saphian of St. Louis. She raised her fry on baby brine shrimp, strained through a handkerchief to obtain the smallest particles. White worms, beefheart and gammarus were fed to her breeders.

Many formulas are offered to the breeder trying to raise the fry away from the parents. The majority of these formulas use powdered egg yolk with additives. Since it is impossible to duplicate the slime produced by the parents, only an acceptable substitute can be used.

The following is a somewhat time-consuming method which the authors recommend for raising the fry artificially. Often a few batches of fry will be lost until the aquarist gains experience in the technique. The formula consists of powdered egg yolk which is available from a baker. Regular egg yolk is too dry and crumbly, while powdered egg yolk is sticky and holds together when moistened.

After the eggs have been laid, wait two hours until all the eggs have had the opportunity to become fertilized. At this time, remove the eggs and place them in water that has been aged twenty-four hours or that has been taken from the parents' tank. Keep the temperature the same as that of the parents' tank. Place an airstone in front of the slate with the eggs. Some type of fungus retardant must be added to the tank. Methylene blue and acriflavine are suitable. For acriflavine, make a solution of seven 200 mg. tablets dissolved in a half gallon of distilled water. Add one and a half tablespoons of this solution to each gallon of water. Acriflavine in the concentration listed does not sterilize discus. If it did, one of the authors' entire breeding stocks would have been made useless.

In three days the fry will become wigglers. At this point remove them from the tank and place them in aged water. Keep an airstone going and raise the temperature to 87^0 F. This increases the metabolism of the young fry and will encourage them to eat. It will take three more days for the fry to become free-swimming. When they reach this stage, wait four hours before proceeding to the next step so that any traces of egg in their egg sacs are absorbed.

Now the aquarist can begin feeding the yolk. Mix four ounces of powdered egg yolk with one package of unflavored

THE WORLD'S LARGEST SELECTION OF PET, ANIMAL, AND MUSIC BOOKS.

T.F.H. Publications publishes more than 900 books covering many hobby aspects (dogs, cats, birds, fish, small animals, music, etc.). Whether you are a beginner or an advanced hobbyist you will find exactly what you're looking for among our complete listing of books. For a free catalog fill out the form on the other side of this page and mail it today.

. . CATS . . .

. . . BIRDS . .

. . . DOGS . . .

. . . ANIMALS . . .

. . FISH . . .

. . . MUSIC . . .

For more than 30 years, *Tropical Fish Hobbyist* has been the source of accurate, up-to-the-minute, and fascinating information on every facet of the aquarium hobby.

Join the more than 50,000 devoted readers worldwide who wouldn't miss a single issue.

gelatin. Add a half a teaspoon of agar-agar and half a teaspoon of Metamucil, the latter being used for the prevention of constipation. A shallow pan should be utilized. Smear the egg yolk on the side of the pan. Then fill with an inch of water. This water should be treated with 250 mg. of penicillin to five gallons to hold the bacteria count down. No airstone should be used during this time. The pan should float in a heated tank.

After two hours remove the fry from the feeding pan. This can be done effectively with an eye dropper. Place them in clean aged water at a temperature of 87° F. An airstone should be added to this holding tank. Check to see whether the fry have accepted any egg yolk. Their stomachs should be plump. Clean the feeding pan in preparation for the next feeding. The fry should be fed four times a day but can thrive on three feedings.

After the fifth day the fry can be weaned off the egg yolk and onto live baby brine shrimp. This should be fed twice daily, supplemented with microworms once a day. A 5-gallon tank can hold a hundred or more fry. Make a one-third water change once a week. After three weeks the fry can be given liquefied beefheart and frozen brine shrimp. It must be pointed out that babies raised artificially will not grow as fast as parent-raised discus.

The following is another method which can be used in raising fry. It is easier and less time-consuming. Leave the slate with the parents for two hours so that all the eggs are fertilized. Then place the slate in a 10-gallon tank to which ten drops per gallon of methylene blue have been added. Keep the temperature at 80° F. and use an airstone. The fry will become wigglers in three days and free-swimming in another three. Raise the temperature four to six degrees. Make pancakes from the frozen egg yolk mixture. Take only the amount necessary from the freezer and *never refreeze thawed egg yolk*. Dip a finger in the fry tank water and form a very thin pancake about half an inch in diameter. Float half a

←1

2

3

(1) A mated pair of discus seek out a suitable spawning site which is usually a vertical surface. Photo by Andre Roth. (2) When two discus swim together and tend to remain away from the rest of the fishes in the tank, a pair-bond may be forming. Photo courtesy of *Midori-Shobo* Magazine. (3) These discus fry have just hatched out and still adhere to the spawning substrate. Photo by Andre Roth.

(1) A pair of *Symphysodon aequifasciata* spawning. The female (front) is about to deposit more eggs on the vertical spawning slab. Note her swollen and protruding ovipositor. Photo by Three Lions, Inc. (2) A pair of *S. discus* exhibiting courting behavior. Photo by Mueller-Schmida.

dozen of these in the tank. Hopefully the egg yolk will be consumed. Siphon off the uneaten food. One-third of the water in the tank should be changed twice daily. When changing the water, add 250 mg. of penicillin for each five gallons of water. The water changes will serve as a laxative, much like the Metamucil in the first formula.

In the corner of the tank use a filter with a layer of charcoal on the bottom, then a layer of wool and finally sand. This filter must be changed every day. An alternative is to use a sponge filter. It must have been used on another tank so that it contains some bacteria. The sponge filter will not need to be cleaned or changed. Be careful not to over-aerate. After five days the discus can be fed brine shrimp nauplii twice a day and microworms once a day. This method is not guaranteed to work all the time.

(1) Both the male and female discus remain close to their spawning site during courting and incubation. Photo by Andre Roth. (2) A piece of slate leaned vertically against the side of the aquarium makes an excellent spawning site for discus. Photo by the author. (3, 4) Once the territory is staked out, the discus defends it as vigorously as almost any other cichlid. Photos by Andre Roth.

The true *Symphysodon discus*. Note the broad vertical bar at the center of the body.   Photo by Dietrich. **Below:** The discus breeding tank should have plenty of firm vertical surfaces to give the fish a choice of spawning sites.

Cross-Breeding Discus

It has been observed by the authors that courtship and mating differ slightly from one color variety to another. The greens prefer to spawn at the top of the flower pot or slate, while a pair of Heckels will spawn at the bottom of the slate or on the rim of the flower pot. Some varieties keep their young noticeably clean while others might fan the young to a great degree but never mouth them to clean them. Other varieties move all around the tank, but some color varieties never move while the fry are feeding during the raising of the young. These observations may change from breeder to breeder, of course.

Heckel colors are usually dominant if a red female is spawned with a male Heckel. Most of the fry will inherit the

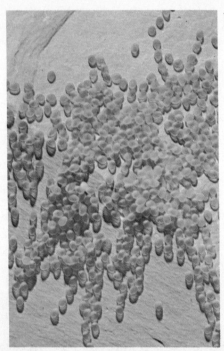

1

3→

(1) A closeup view of discus eggs. At a later stage of development the embryos will be clearly seen atop the large yolk mass. (2) The parent discus rarely leave the immediate vicinity of the spawning site. Photos 1 and 2 by Dr. D. Terver, Nancy Aquarium, France. (3) Through selective breeding, Dr. E. Schmidt-Focke developed this magnificent turquoise discus. Note the rich mahogany background color of this fish. Photo by A.L. Pieter.

2

(1) At four weeks of age baby discus still feed from the parents' body secretions, but they also take other substitute foods at this stage. Photo by Dr. G. Lanyi. (2) At eight weeks of age young discus have nearly completed their metamorphosis into the adult form. Photo by G. Budich.

three stripes from the Heckel parent. Out of a Heckel-red cross which one of the authors raised, 90% of the young had the Heckel stripes—one through the head, one through the middle of the body, one through the tail. Only 10% had characteristics of the mother. Heckels, whether spawned with blue, green, turquoise or cobalt blue discus, etc. are dominant in nine cases out of ten, passing on color and Heckel stripes.

If a blue and green were crossed the young would look intermediate, showing blue and green stripes of different widths and intensities through the head, dorsal and anal. Thus, no two fry would appear the same.

Most discus crosses are stronger and healthier than pure color varieties, because the more desirable traits seem to become dominant when the inbreeding process is disrupted. It might take five to ten years to develop a strain from cross breeding that breeds true. A fine example of this is the cobalt blue, which is a cross between the Heckel and royal blue. The turquoise discus is a cross between the royal blue and Tefe green. A blue-face is a cross between a brown and a blue. These and other crosses are on their way to becoming fresh new varieties that might someday form the backbone of a new discus community.

3

The bright red eyes are one of the most outstanding features of nearly all discus strains. In light-colored stains such as the powder blue discus (1) and the brown discus (2) the red eyes stand out quite boldly. Photos courtesy of *Midori-Shobo* Magazine. (3) The red eye even carries into the albino strain and seems brighter because of the fish's complete lack of dark pigments. Photo by Jiri Taborsky.

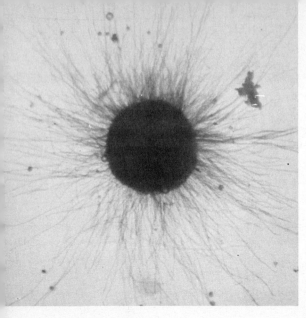

Fungus growing on a dead fish egg. The tiny dark spots are fungal spores. Photo by Dr. C. Emmens. **Below:** *Hexamita,* a flagellated protozoan. Certain *Hexamita* species have been associated with hole-in-the-head disease, a common malady of discus. Photo by Dr. H. Reichenbach-Klinke.

Diseases

Discus can be besieged with many diseases; however, with proper care and conditions, it is not difficult to raise healthy discus. Some fish hobbyists often discourage would-be discus enthusiasts from buying discus, since they might not have had luck with raising their own discus. Do not be put off by these people. Raising discus is a worthwhile challenge.

The following are some of the diseases you might (let us emphasize *might*) encounter with the discus.

BLOAT

If an adult discus (or any other fish, for that matter) is overfed, it will develop a deadly bloat. The stomach will

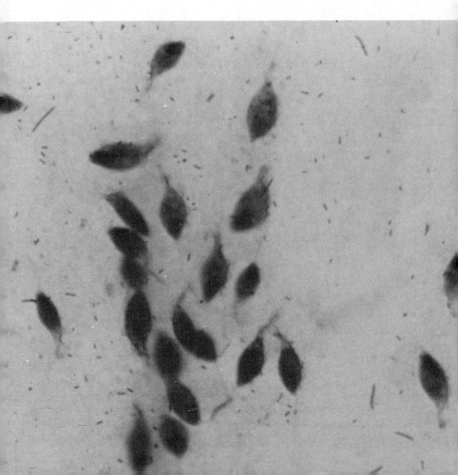

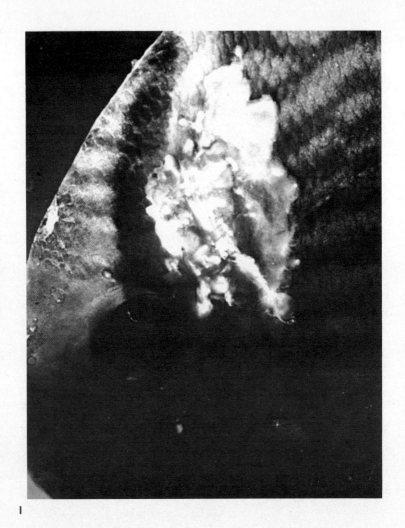

I

(1) The festering sores on the head of this discus are the result of hole-in-the-head disease. The recommended treatment is an internal dose of a drug called Flagyl. External baths of any medication are rarely effective against this disease. (2) A highly magnified view of *Hexamita* (the elongate, flagellated bodies). These organisms are believed to be the cause of hole-in-the-head disease, a disease also known by the name hexamitiasis. Photos by Dr. H. Reichenbach-Klinke. (3) Fish eggs attacked and destroyed by fungus. Brooding discus parents usually pick fungused eggs out of the clutch, and that helps prevent the fungus from spreading to healthy eggs. Photo by Frickhinger.

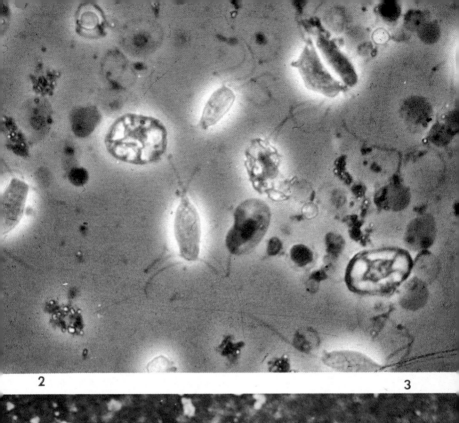

swell as if it were full of eggs. Once this problem is advanced, the fish will most likely die. Since the discus swells with body liquids, only mild cases can be successfully cured.

Cure: Use one Kanulase tablet per five gallons of water per day. Change half the water daily for a week. Keep tank dark while treating. Do not feed fish. Keep water temperature about 79° F.

POPEYE

With this disease the back of the eye fills with pus and swells to the point where the eye appears to dislodge. Sometimes it does. Dissolved gases in the water and too much heat are to blame for this condition. If the eye appears to be beyond saving, lancing the back of it sometimes can provide a miracle, but on a whole it is a dangerous remedy.

Cure: Swab the eye with a solution of three tablespoons of non-iodized salt per quart. Add one copper sponge per 50-gallon tank of water. Make a one-third water change twice a week.

SCALE LOSS

This "disease" is often observed in wild fish from South America. They are sometimes bagged together, thereby scratching each other with their dorsals. A fish can also contract this ailment by being scratched in some other manner. The scales on the sides of the fish fall out, leaving a bloody tint. After the scales protrude and fall out, fungus sets in.

Cure: Prevention is the best cure. When receiving discus, be sure they are packed individually. If this is not possible, add one tablet of Chloromycetin per ten gallons of water upon arrival. If sores are already present, swab them with Mercurochrome (50%). Another cure is to use one copper sponge and add two drops of formalin per gallon to a 50-gallon tank. Another alternative is to add one tablet of Chloromycetin per ten gallons for three days; then change one-third of the water.

FLUKES

Flukes are found in very many wild discus and in a good percentage of tank-raised fish which have been fed live foods. Flukes are actually trematode worms that flourish in the gills of the fish. There is not an intermediate host. No snails are involved. If left untreated, this problem will almost always kill the fish. The larvae destroy the gill membranes, and the fish suffocates. Rapid breathing, loss of color and closed fins are characteristics of this type of infection.

Cure: Administer two drops of formaldehyde per gallon per day for two days. Also add five drops per gallon of methylene blue. Be sure there is proper aeration when treating with formaldehyde. A formaldehyde bath might also work. Place the discus in a tank for five minutes to which twenty drops of formaldehyde per gallon have been added—but watch closely to see whether the discus shows any signs of distress. If this occurs, remove the fish promptly.

FIN FUNGUS

This disease causes the fins to develop a small white growth at the tip of the fins. Usually fish get it when they are moved. It is often found on newly received wild discus.

Cure: Heat is the best cure for fin fungus. Raise the temperature to 90° F. for a few days. If it gets worse, take the fish out and cut the infected part off. Swab with methylene blue or acriflavine.

HAIRWORMS

Hairworms are usually found in wild discus. However, since many angelfish, including tank-raised angels, are infested with hairworms, they may be transferred from an angel tank to the discus by using the same equipment.

Cure: These worms are sensitive to heat; therefore, raise the temperature to 100 degrees for two days. The discus can tolerate the heat long enough for the worms to be destroyed. Another cure is to add four mg. of Dylox to one gallon of water.

(1) Discus weakened by poor environmental conditions are subject to attack by digenetic trematode larvae. Photo by Frickhinger. (2) Aneurysms in fish gills can be caused by toxic ammonia in the water. Photo courtesy of C.E. Smith, U.S.F.W.S. (3) Fungal growth on the body of a discus. Fungi can attack any open sore or wound; such attacks are usually considered to be secondary infections. Copyright 1979 by Wardley Products Co. (4) *Capillaria* species (hairworms) are more common in wild discus than in domesticated strains. Photo by Dr. H. Reichenbach-Klinke.

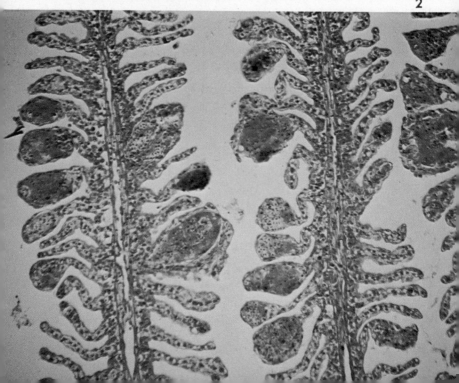

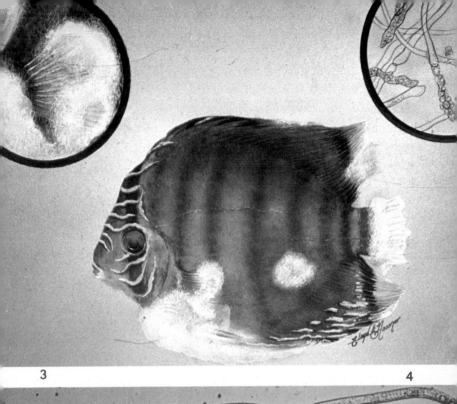

2

3

4

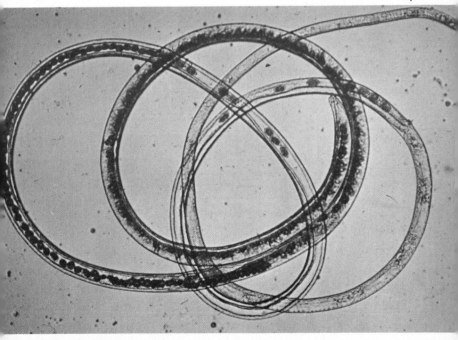

TUBERCULOSIS

This disease has afflicted discus coming from Southeast Asia in the past few years. The bacilli attack the organs and destroy them. Constant high temperatures are believed to favor the spread of tuberculosis in fish. There is no known cure.

CONSTIPATION

Constipation is not uncommon in discus; young fry, which are almost always eating, are especially susceptible. It is the result of overfeeding.

Cure: A salt bath can be an effective remedy. Cease feeding the discus for a few days when constipation develops. It is advisable to fast the discus once a week to prevent this condition. The addition of a copper sponge per 50-gallon tank can be beneficial.

SWIM BLADDER DISEASE

When a fish develops this disease, it might have difficulty swimming. It falls head over tail and can't maintain itself on an even level. It may also lie flat on the aquarium floor. The trouble is caused by poor diet, sudden water changes and pressure or temperature changes. Overfeeding might also be a contributing factor.

Cure: Fish seldom recover. If the discus does recover, chances are it will be crippled.

WHIRLING DISEASE

The fish loses equilibrium and whirls about dizzily. It cannot maintain itself in a normal swimming position. It is caused by a protozoan *(Lentospora cerebralis)*. By the time the fish begins to whirl, the disease has already penetrated the cartilages of the skull and destroyed that part of the brain which controls the balancing power of the fish.

Cure: There is no known cure since the organism is deeply imbedded in the brain. Destroy the fish and sterilize all equipment.

SHOCK

This is similar to shimmying in livebearers. It is caused by drastic temperature and pH changes.

Cure: Prevention again is the best cure. Keep discus at a steady temperature and pH, especially when moving to a new tank.

PARASITIC ISOPODS

This problem, caused by an isopod, *Artystone trysibia,* is found almost entirely in discus in the wild. Only very rarely does it develop in a tank-raised fish. The affected fish has a tendency to hide and swims erratically.

Cure: Recently a Heckel which had *Artystone trysibia* in its left side was observed by the authors. The decision was made to try to remove the isopod. The fish was taken out of the tank and kept wet. Tweezers were used to remove the isopod, and an antibiotic was applied to the sore. After two days two more isopods were observed and removed in the same manner. However, this time the fish was injected with penicillin and placed in a 20-gallon tank which was also treated with penicillin. The fish darkened slightly and swam. However, it refused food and on the sixth day it died. Penicillin had been added to the water daily. Therefore, the fish could have succumbed to an overdose of medication and not to the parasites or their effects.

HUNGER STRIKES

Discus often go on hunger strikes. They are caused by poor feeding habits or long intervals without foods. When a collector in the wild catches discus, he doesn't bother feeding them, since they will be shipped within a short time. When the fish finally arrive in the hobbyist's tank, their appetite is deadened.

Cure: Several methods can be combined to induce the discus to resume eating. Raise the temperature from 82º F. to 88-90º F. This should increase their metabolism. The acidity

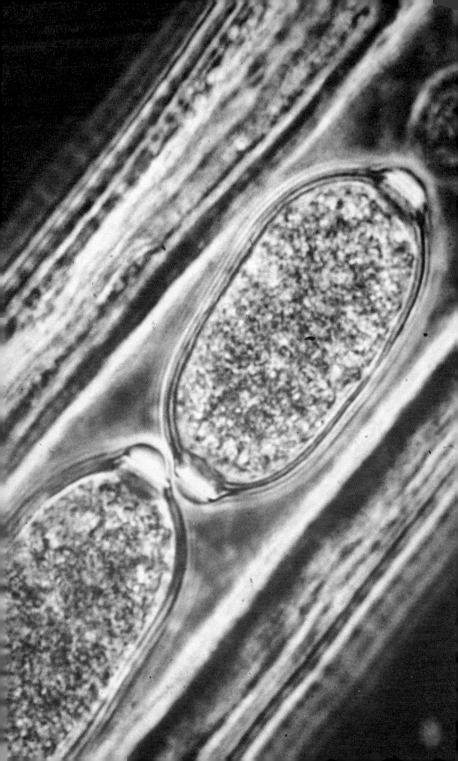

(1) Eggs of a hairworm (*Capillaria* species) found in the liver of a fish. Photo by Frickhinger. (2) There are many kinds of copepods that can attach themselves to a fish's gills. Photo by Frickhinger. (3) Acid-fast bacteria in a kidney smear from a tropical fish with tuberculosis. Photo courtesy of Piscean Ltd.

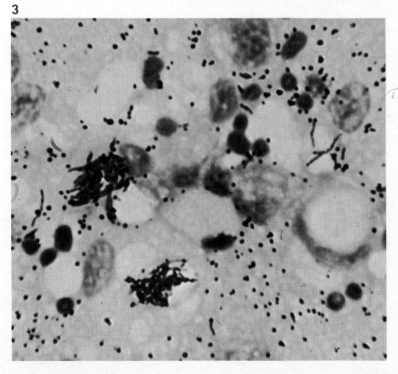

of the water should be increased slightly also. If this fails, introduce a discus that has a hearty appetite into the tank. Seeing that another discus will eat sometimes will encourage the fasting discus to break its hunger strike. As a last resort, feed the discus white worms or tubifex worms, even though the latter is very undesirable. Switch to beefheart as soon as possible.

HEADWORMS OR HOLE-IN-THE-HEAD DISEASE

This disease is not actually a worm but a pus discharge from the head caused by bacteria. For many years, aquarists have claimed headworms are caused by live tubifex worms or live mosquito larvae which contain an abundance of bacteria. This theory should not be ruled out as a possibility, but some experiments have shown that discus which have never been fed the above-mentioned foods still contract the disease. In our opinion, it is caused by bacteria in the water due to spoiled food.

Characteristic of the disease is a pus discharge around the head area, generally above the mouth, around the forehead and in back of the eye. In very severe cases, it extends to the lateral line. At first, the fish begins to turn dark and will stop eating, thereby losing weight rapidly. At times the fish will continually face either the top or bottom of the tank. Crater-like holes develop; these holes will after two or three days discharge pus. The holes rarely close, even if the fish recovers. If not treated, the discus will die.

Cure: There are several courses of treatments that can be recommended for the disease. Raising the temperature from 85⁰ to 90⁰ F. should stop the pus discharge temporarily. The use of antibiotics such as Zeemax, Myracin and Furanace works very well. Add the prescribed dosage to the water or incorporate in the food. Mercurochrome (50%) pushed into the craters can also be beneficial.

One of the latest treatments the authors utilized is to mix 250 mg. of Flagyl with the food. Dissolve a capsule in a cup of water and add to a pound of beefheart. If the discus refuses to eat, the dissolved solution should be added right to the tank. Use 250 mg. for every ten gallons of water. Keep the temperature at 90⁰ F. for a week and stop treatment. Allow the temperature to remain at 90⁰ F. for another two weeks.

It is usually evident that a discus is ailing if it stops eating, turns dark or swims in an uncharacteristic manner. Some discus (such as the Heckel) almost always have three black bars present, but when the nine bars are continually apparent there is something wrong with the fish.

Often the discus will succumb to the faulty methods used in the treatment of an ailment rather than the disease itself. For example, in a 50-gallon tank with gravel, filters, plants, pot or slate, there actually are about 30 to 35 gallons of water. The aquarist treats the tank as if it contained a full 50 gallons, however, so it follows that the discus will receive a hearty overdose, perhaps enough to kill it. Be careful in administering the dosage when treating discus.

Spironucleus taken from the gut of a discus. Infected fishes usually have whitish, thread-like feces that don't drop off very readily. Photo by Dr. G. Schubert.

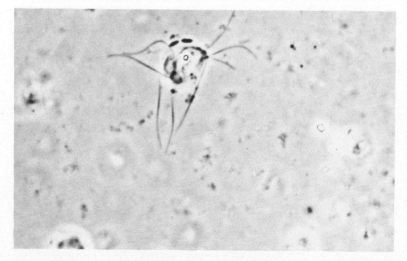